Thinking Matters, LLC
704 Gregg St
Nashville, MI 49073
admin@thinkingmatters.us

Thinking Matters Evolution Volume 2

For Decision Making

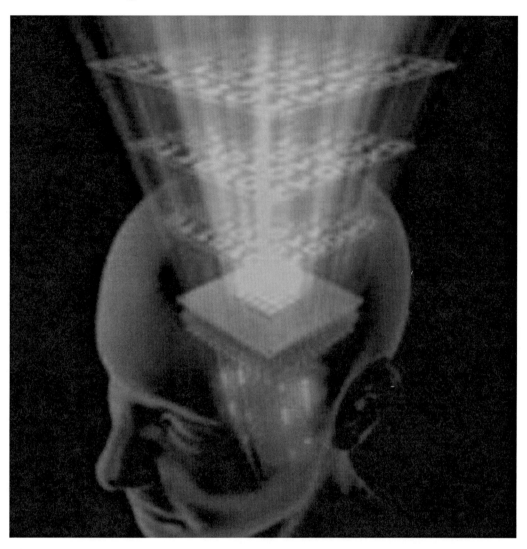

Participant Workbook

Step one: Decision Descriptions

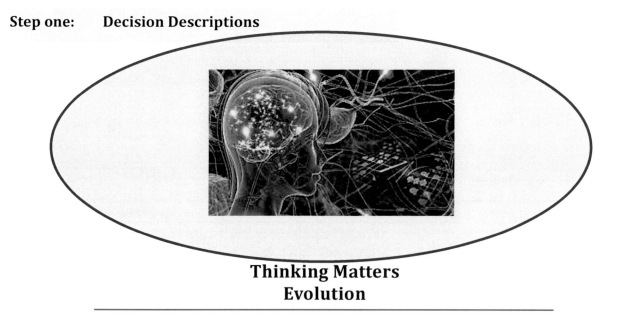

**Thinking Matters
Evolution**

Step one of *Thinking Matters Evolution for Decision Making* helps us separate the decision to be made from our emotional reaction to the situation. The skill of seeing the difference between our viewpoint and the facts helps us to see our own responsibility and leads to setting a goal. It also, helps us to slow down our thinking and consider choices we might not have considered before. Reacting quickly to emotional responses often helps people make decisions that get us into trouble and harm others.

Thinking Matters Evolution for Decision Making helps me to become more aware of how my thinking leads toward decisions. Too often it appears as if the outside world interferes with what I am trying to do. When this happens I sometimes feel frustrated, angry or powerless. This usually helps me feel anxious and respond as if the situation demands my immediate response.

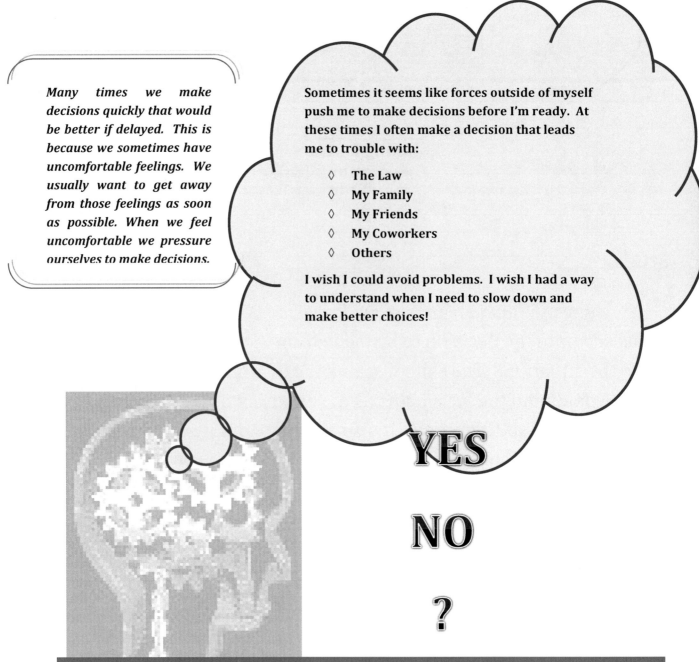

Many times we make decisions quickly that would be better if delayed. This is because we sometimes have uncomfortable feelings. We usually want to get away from those feelings as soon as possible. When we feel uncomfortable we pressure ourselves to make decisions.

Sometimes it seems like forces outside of myself push me to make decisions before I'm ready. At these times I often make a decision that leads me to trouble with:

◊   **The Law**
◊   **My Family**
◊   **My Friends**
◊   **My Coworkers**
◊   **Others**

I wish I could avoid problems. I wish I had a way to understand when I need to slow down and make better choices!

YES

NO

?

*Do we sometimes make decisions without thinking things through clearly? Are there times when we involve ourselves in situations that we don't really need to? Do our emotions sometimes put pressure on us to act quickly when it isn't **necessary** to act quickly? Can we understand how our feelings (emotions/physical sensations) help us make decisions? Is how we appear to others important to us?*

The first thing I can do is to list situations where I think I need to make a decision. I will make a list of seven situations from the past where I wish I could have made better choices and not gotten into trouble or hurt myself or someone else. Write them as if you're in the situation *now*.

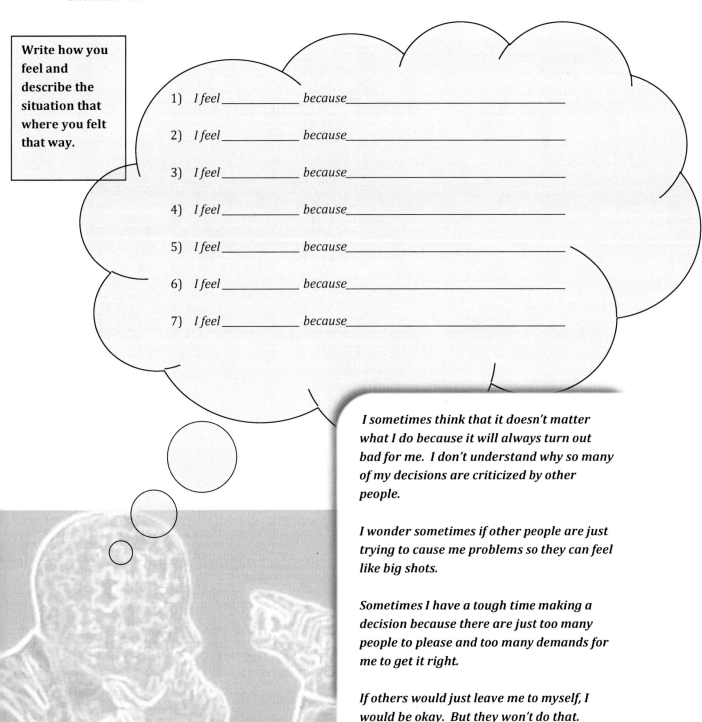

Write how you feel and describe the situation that where you felt that way.

1) *I feel*_____ *because*_____

2) *I feel*_____ *because*_____

3) *I feel*_____ *because*_____

4) *I feel*_____ *because*_____

5) *I feel*_____ *because*_____

6) *I feel*_____ *because*_____

7) *I feel*_____ *because*_____

I sometimes think that it doesn't matter what I do because it will always turn out bad for me. I don't understand why so many of my decisions are criticized by other people.

I wonder sometimes if other people are just trying to cause me problems so they can feel like big shots.

Sometimes I have a tough time making a decision because there are just too many people to please and too many demands for me to get it right.

If others would just leave me to myself, I would be okay. But they won't do that.

It's not easy to figure out how my thinking helps me make decisions. How do all of these thoughts and feelings fit together?

Thinking Matters Evolution for Decision Making can help me look at situations in different ways. I can choose how I *want* to feel about a certain situation and then decide what action to take to help me feel that way.

Pick a situation from your list of seven and use it on this work sheet. Write four different decisions you could make and how those decisions would help you feel.

Avoid words like "better", "worse", "positive" or "negative".

The emotions you write should words like:

- **Angry**
- **Encouraged**
- **Sad**
- **Powerful**

1) I will feel _____ if I decide to

_____.

2) I will feel _____ if I decide to

_____.

I sometimes don't think very much about how I want to feel or how I want things to turn out.

At these times I start to believe I don't have many choices or don't take time to see all of my choices.

Some choices could make things better for me and others. Some choices can make things worse.

How can I know what to choose?

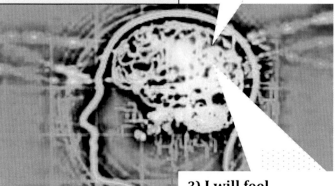

3) I will feel _____ if I decide to

_____.

4) I will feel _____ if I decide to

_____.

Do I often make a list of my choices before making an important decision? What types of decision do I think are important? How do I know the difference between important decisions and unimportant decisions? Are there times when What others say makes a decision seem more important than I really think it is? Do I consider how others will view me when making decisions?

From the previous page:

Write in:
Box 1) the decision that you think is *the best choice*

Box 2) the decision you think is *the second best choice.*

1)_____

_____

_____

_____

What does it sound like when I write a decision? Is there any:

◊   **Blame**
◊   **Excuses**
◊   **Accusations**
◊   **Minimizing**
◊   **Omission**
◊   **Exaggeration**

How do these things help me make a decision? Do they help me view myself as RIGHT? Do I think I deserve something and others disagree?

2)_____

_____

_____

_____

If I think it is acceptable to do something, does it become more or less likely that I will do it? If I am thinking it is my right to act in a certain way, how likely is it that I will stop myself? What things can I think or say to myself that will help me look at situations with a feeling of righteousness? Can I say things in a certain way to make it sound as if I have a right to do something? Can I decide that others are wrong and use that to make decisions?

I know there are consequences for other people when I make decisions. If I think about consequences for those people I might make better decisions. Maybe this will help me have better relationships and avoid trouble.

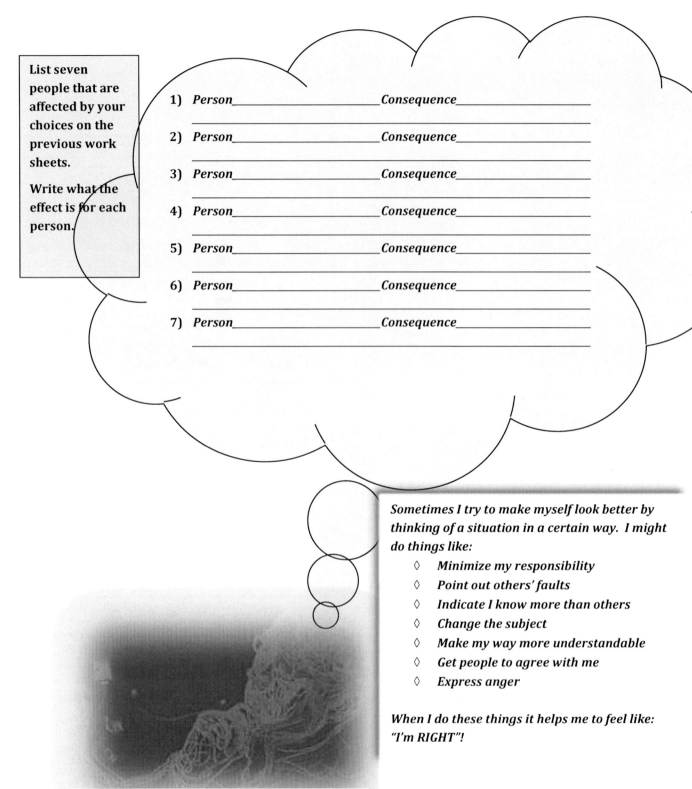

List seven people that are affected by your choices on the previous work sheets.

Write what the effect is for each person.

1) Person_____Consequence_____
   _____

2) Person_____Consequence_____
   _____

3) Person_____Consequence_____
   _____

4) Person_____Consequence_____
   _____

5) Person_____Consequence_____
   _____

6) Person_____Consequence_____
   _____

7) Person_____Consequence_____
   _____

Sometimes I try to make myself look better by thinking of a situation in a certain way. I might do things like:

- ◊ *Minimize my responsibility*
- ◊ *Point out others' faults*
- ◊ *Indicate I know more than others*
- ◊ *Change the subject*
- ◊ *Make my way more understandable*
- ◊ *Get people to agree with me*
- ◊ *Express anger*

When I do these things it helps me to feel like: "I'm RIGHT"!

I can consider whoever I want to. I can also, leave them out of my decisions. It is MY choice.

Objective viewpoints are when I focus only on what *I* did. I don't say *why* I did it or what role *others had* in the situation. I try to remember that I am responsible for my own behavior. I can separate my reasons for doing something from my action if I decide to.

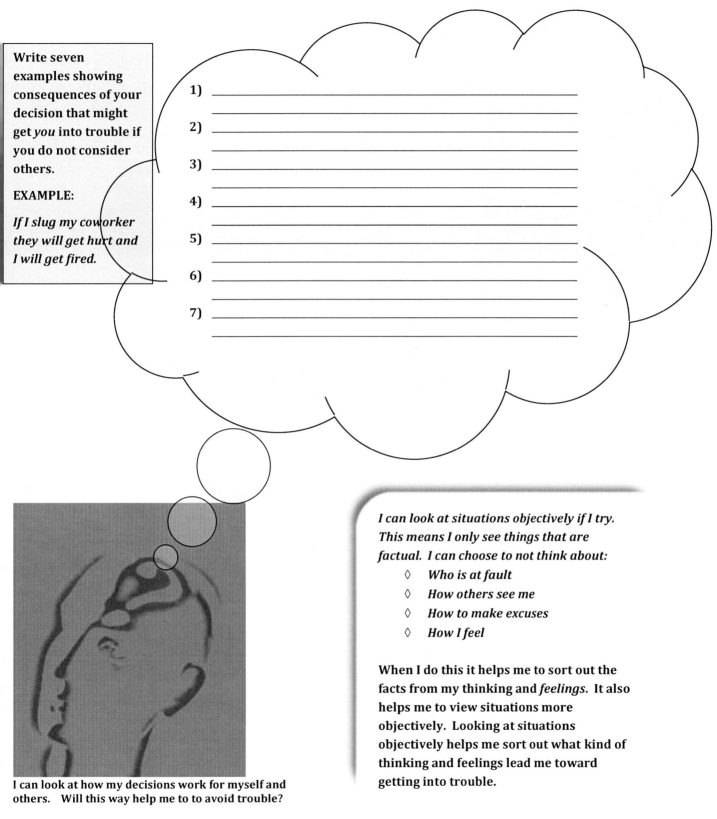

Write seven examples showing consequences of your decision that might get *you* into trouble if you do not consider others.

EXAMPLE:

If I slug my coworker they will get hurt and I will get fired.

1) _____
_____
2) _____
_____
3) _____
_____
4) _____
_____
5) _____
_____
6) _____
_____
7) _____
_____

I can look at how my decisions work for myself and others. Will this way help me to to avoid trouble?

I can look at situations objectively if I try. This means I only see things that are factual. I can choose to not think about:
- ◊ *Who is at fault*
- ◊ *How others see me*
- ◊ *How to make excuses*
- ◊ *How I feel*

When I do this it helps me to sort out the facts from my thinking and *feelings*. It also helps me to view situations more objectively. Looking at situations objectively helps me sort out what kind of thinking and feelings lead me toward getting into trouble.

Notes:

Notes:

Step two:

Pieces of the Puzzle

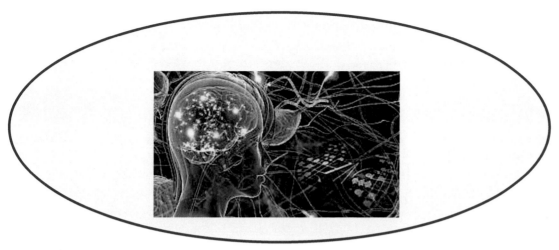

Thinking Matters
Evolution

Step 2 of *Thinking Matters Evolution for Decision Making* helps us to find the pieces of the puzzle that is our decision making. What we believe to be true, our thoughts, feelings and past experiences help us see things the way we see them. If we find the different pieces and see how they fit together we can make better decisions that lead us away from trouble and/or harming others.

Thinking Matters Evolution for Decision Making helps me to become more aware of how my thinking leads toward decisions. Too often is seems like things just happen without me thinking about it! I can't always make sense of how the situation developed and don't know just what to do to avoid the same kind of trouble in the future.

We have all been in situations where our behavior led us to trouble. Sometimes we look back and ask ourselves, "What made me do that?"

We sometimes have good reasons for what we do when we get into trouble. But good reasons are not always enough to help us avoid trouble.

Sometimes it seems like I would not get into trouble as much if others would quit forcing me to make decisions I don't want to make. I wish I could avoid problems with:

◊ *The Law*
◊ *My family*
◊ *My friends*
◊ *My Coworkers*
◊ *Others*

I wish others would focus on the good things I do and not pay so much attention to my mistakes

YES

NO

?

Do we keep secrets because we think we will be wrongly judged? Do we try to make sure other people have opinions about us that are favorable? Do we sometimes try to convince ourselves that we deserve things we haven't earned? Do we sometimes fool ourselves in the process and make bad decisions?

I will write down four decisions I think I will need to make in the future. I will pick two situations that I want to use as practice for avoiding trouble in the future. All of my situations will start with the word "I".

Put a star (*) by the situations you want to work with. Keep them objective. Don't use words that point blame or make excuses

1)   I need/want to _____

because_____

2)   I need/want to _____

because_____

3)   I need/want to _____

because_____

4)   I need/want to _____

because_____

I wonder if I make poor decisions sometimes because I just want to feel better and more in control. Can I change that?

I sometimes look at situations and play a mental movie of how I think things will turn out.

Sometimes I'm right. Other times I find out later that I didn't have enough facts. Not having enough information helps me make decisions that turn out poorly for me and others.

Maybe I should look deeper into my mental movies to see if I know enough or if I should gather more information.

Decision Description #1: _____

My Thoughts

1) _____
_____
2) _____
_____
3) _____
_____

Pick a situation where you put a star (*).

1) Write the situation in the box provided

2) Write down six thoughts you have about the decision.

I can see the thoughts that I use exactly as they happen in a situation. It will take some work and practice. When I do this it can help me sort out the thinking that leads me to trouble.

If I view the situation in my mind like I'm watching a movie. This sometimes makes it easier for me to remember my thoughts and feelings.

I can use this practice to understand how my decisions are made. I can also become more aware of the puzzle of my thinking and feelings.

4) _____
_____
5) _____
_____
6) _____
_____

How often are we aware of which thoughts help us make decisions? Do we really pay very much attention to our thoughts as they happen? Will we learn more about ourselves if we learn to separate our thoughts from the facts? How does the way we think about something or someone help us make a decision?

Decision Description #1: _____

| My Feelings/Emotions |

1)_____
_____
2)_____
_____
3)_____
_____

Write the same situation at the top of this work sheet.

1) Write down the thoughts again from the previous page

2) Write down the emotions you feel when you have the thought.

Sometimes it is hard to separate thinking from emotions. This is why it is important to look at thoughts AND feelings. We can begin to see how our thinking helps us feel good or bad, better or worse.

Whatever feelings come to mind first are probably the ones that should be written down. Sometimes we think of other thoughts and feelings that we forgot about as we practice.

It is very important to be honest with ourselves.

4)_____
_____
5)_____
_____
6)_____
_____

If it makes me feel good or better when I think about doing something, am I more likely to do it? How do our feelings/emotions help us make a decision? Do we have physical sensations that help us make decisions?

Decision Description #2: _____

My Thoughts

1) _____

_____

2) _____

_____

3) _____

_____

Pick the other situation where you put a star (*).

1) Write the situation in the box provided

2) Write down six thoughts you have about the decision.

I can see the thoughts that I use exactly as they happen in a situation. It will take some work and practice. When I do this it can help me sort out the thinking that leads me to trouble.

If I view the situation in my mind like I'm watching a movie. This sometimes makes it easier for me to remember my thoughts and feelings.

I can use this practice to understand how my decisions are made. I can also become more aware of the puzzle of my thinking and feelings.

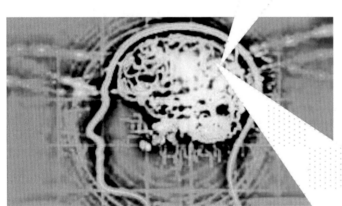

4) _____

_____

5) _____

_____

6) _____

_____

How often are we aware of which thoughts help us make decisions? Do we really pay very much attention to our thoughts as they happen? Will we learn more about ourselves if we learn to separate our thoughts from the facts? How does the way we think about something or someone help us make a decision?

Decision Description #2: _____

My Feelings/Emotions ⟶

1)_____
_____

2)_____
_____

3)_____
_____

From the previous sheet write the same situation at the top of this work sheet.

1) Write down the thought again

2) Write down the emotions you feel when you have the thought.

Sometimes it is hard to separate thinking from emotions. This is why it is important to look at thoughts AND feelings. We can begin to see how our thinking helps us feel good or bad, better or worse.

Whatever feelings come to mind first are probably the ones that should be written down. Sometimes we think of other thoughts and feelings that we forgot about as we practice.

It is very important to be honest with ourselves.

4)_____
_____

5)_____
_____

6)_____
_____

If it makes me feel good or better when I think about doing something, am I more likely to do it? How do our feelings/emotions help us make a decision? Do we have physical sensations that help us make decisions?

Notes:

Notes:

Notes:

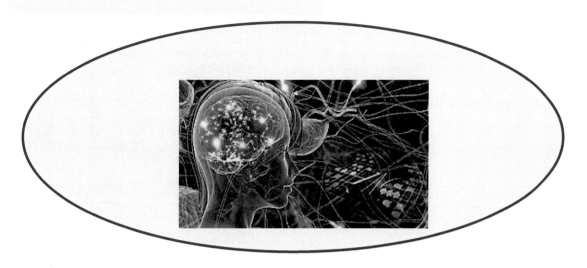

Thinking Matters
Evolution

Step 3 of *Thinking Matters Evolution for Decision Making* helps us look for the thinks we usually leave out when making decisions. This is important because we develop habits that seem reasonable and normal. Unfortunately, some of these thinking habits help us make decisions we later regret. Step 3 provides practice looking f important pieces we sometimes forget to think about when making decisions.

Thinking Matters Evolution helps me to become more aware of what thinking helps me make decisions. Sometimes it seems like my reaction to situations make sense but still lead me toward trouble. I'm not always sure what I'm missing. I want to avoid the same kind of trouble in the future.

My decisions get me into trouble more often than many other people I know. I'm not exactly sure how that works.

Different people must see the same situation differently. Maybe I could stay away from trouble more often if I think about some different things before I decide what to do.

Sometimes it seems like I should make different choices. But this is usually *after it's too late.* Looking back at some situations I think about different ways to do things. But by then it's too late.

I wish I could avoid problems with:

◊   The Law
◊   My family
◊   My friends
◊   My Coworkers
◊   Others

I wish I could see better *choices before I make mistakes.*

YES

NO

?

Do we sometimes limit our own choices because it's a lot of work to think things through? Do we sometimes decide to do something because we are embarrassed or feel put-down? Do we always consider many choices before acting? Or, do we often decide right away to "get it over with"?

I will write down the seven situations I wish I could get a "do-over" for. These are situationa I think I could have made better decisions if I had considered more information than I did at the time. I will focus on my decisions and my actiona without trying to make someone else look bad.

Write down seven decisions you made that you think you could have done better with more information. Put a(*) by the two situations you want to work with on the next worksheets

1_)_I_____
_____

2)_I_____
_____

3)_I_____
_____

4)_I_____
_____

5)_I_____
_____

6)_I_____
_____

7)_I_____
_____

It's not easy to figure out how my thinking helps me make decisions. How do all of these thoughts and feelings fit together?

Is it possible for me to consider every little detail of every situation? That seems impossible!

Maybe I can practice looking for the types of information I usually forget to look for. That might make gathering more information a lot faster for me.

If I can look at thing before I make a decision and find new ways of seeing the situation, I might be able to make better decisions.

Situation:_____
_____

1)_____
_____

What did I need to know before I acted?

2)_____
_____

3)_____
_____

Pick a situation where you put a star (*).

1) Write the situation

2) Write down six things you think would have been important to know at the time that you didn't think about.

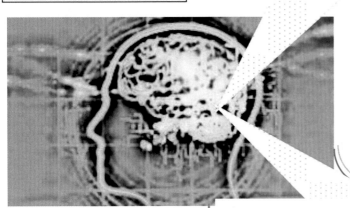

There are many different things I hoped for or want in different situations. It could be what I wanted others to do or say. It could also be how I wanted to feel.

I might have wanted others to view me in a certain way. Or, I might have wanted others to not see me in a certain way.

Maybe I wanted to see myself in a certain way. Or, I might have wanted to avoid feelings that are unpleasant and uncomfortable for me.

I won't be concerned with what order they happened. I need to practice understanding what I wanted from doing the behavior.

4)_____
_____

5)_____
_____

6)_____
_____

Is it possible that the way my beliefs connect to my wants and needs helps me get into trouble? Do I sometimes expect others to see things my way when I have conflict? Do I sometimes expect people to stay out of my way without thinking of what they are trying to accomplish? Do I decide what I want and then figure out that it is right? How do I decide to do whatever it takes to achieve my goal? Will my goals sometimes conflict with what others want? Do I feel powerful and energetic when I have conflict? Do I like feeling powerful and energetic?

Situation:_____
_____

| What did I need to know before I acted? | 1)_____ |

1)_____
_____

2)_____
_____

3)_____
_____

At the top of this work sheet write the *other* situation you chose.

Write down six things you think would have been important to know at the time that you didn't think about'

Sometimes I find it useful to compare two different situations that caused me trouble. I can look at how similar my wants and expectations are when I do this.

Sometimes this can be unpleasant for me. This is because things can seem very different when I am looking back and my interests are not at stake as much.

That's okay. I will just make a mental note that it makes me uncomfortable and try to understand.

4)_____
_____

5)_____
_____

6)_____
_____

If I put what I want ahead of what others want, will I be likely to have more conflict? Will others be more (or less) likely to help me get what I want if the process has conflict? Is it so important that I get what I want that I am willing to get into trouble or hurt myself or others? Do I like conflict because it makes me feel more in charge? Is it easier to just go for it than to slow down and think things through more?

Situation:_____

_____

On the lines provided, write a description of how your decision would have been better for you and others using the new information for the first situation.

_____
_____
_____
_____
_____
_____
_____
_____
_____
_____
_____
_____

Sometimes we know what we want. But, we don't often spend much time considering the effect this has on our decisions. Sometimes when we react quickly to things that are important to us we can make decisions that get us into trouble.

If we practice looking for more information, we can make better decisions. Sometimes we think there isn't enough time to look fo more information. But sometimes, we create more problems by being in a hurry.

My expectations of what I should have and how I should feel are important to me. How does what I expect from myself and others help me make decisions?

Situation:_____
_____

On the lines provided, write a description of how your decision would have been better for you and others using the new information for the first situation.

_____
_____
_____
_____
_____
_____
_____
_____
_____
_____
_____
_____
_____
_____
_____
_____

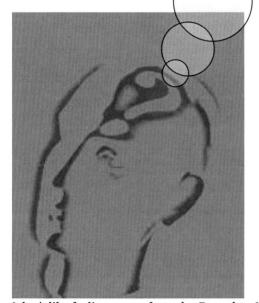

I don't like feeling uncomfortanle. But, when I avoid uncomfortable feelings I seem to get into trouble more often. What is more important to me?

Sometimes when I feel embarrassed or uncomfortable I decide it is someone else's fault. At these times I want them to feel uncomfortable too. I might want to embarrass them or make them feel powerless.

I might want to teach them a lesson *or show them that I will stand up for myself. I might want to rebel against injustice or make others leave me alone.*

If I use these ideas to make decisions, will my decisions be better for everyone or not?

Notes:

Notes:

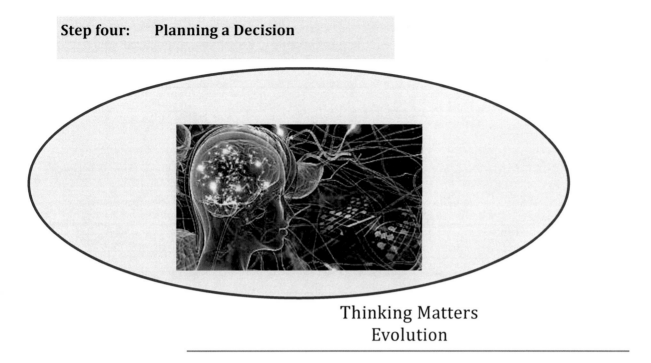

Thinking Matters
Evolution

Step 4 of *Thinking Matters Evolution for Decision Making* helps us look ahead to a decision we will make and plan for it to have the best result. It becomes more comfortable making important decisions when we practice planning.

Thinking Matters Evolution helps me to become more aware of how make important decisions. Sometimes it seems like everything happens all-at-once! I'm not always sure how I decide on something. I want to make better decisions and avoid the same kind trouble in the future.

Sometimes it seems almost like I never even made a decision. Things sort of took on a life of their own.

When this happens people sometimes ask me why I did that. Most of those times, I can't give them an honest answer.

It just seems like there was no choice.

Sometimes it seems like things happen so fast. It's like I didn't even make a decision. It looks to me like something just creates an outcome and now I'm in trouble. It is almost like the decision was made without my input or there was no choice.

I wish I could avoid problems with:

◊ *The Law*
◊ *My family*
◊ *My friends*
◊ *My Coworkers*
◊ *Others*

I wish I could have more control of my decision making. I want to choose my behavior intentionally and not be pulled along by events.

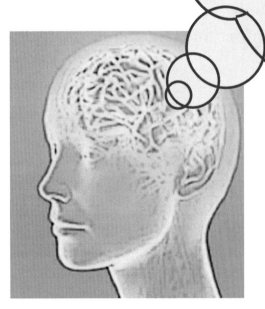

YES

NO

?

Do we ever make decisions we wish we could do over? What kind of decisions are they?

I will write down situations where I will likely need to make an important decision in the future. I will use these situations to practice a way to plan for decisions I will need to make.

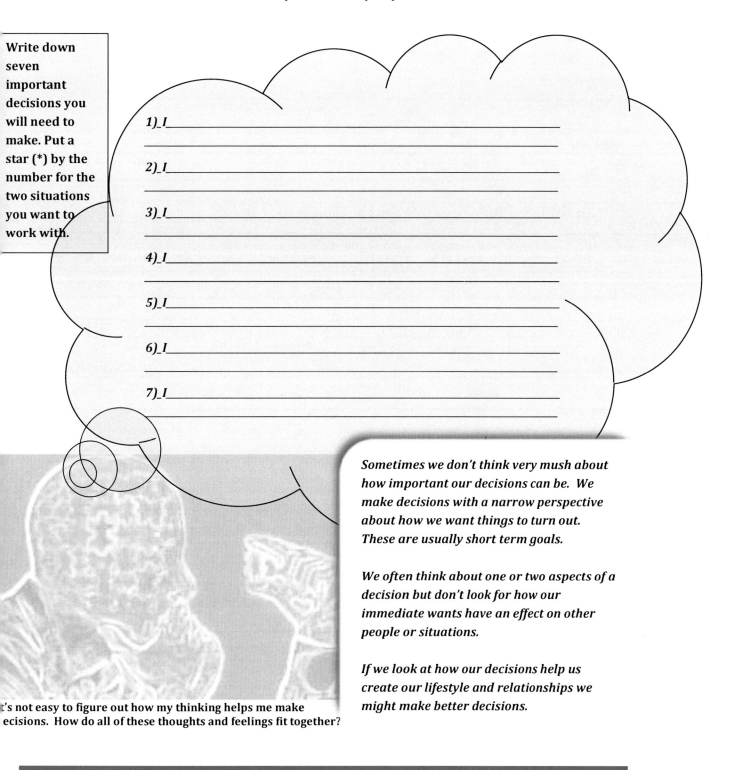

Write down seven important decisions you will need to make. Put a star (*) by the number for the two situations you want to work with.

1)_I_____

_____

2)_I_____

_____

3)_I_____

_____

4)_I_____

_____

5)_I_____

_____

6)_I_____

_____

7)_I_____

_____

Sometimes we don't think very mush about how important our decisions can be. We make decisions with a narrow perspective about how we want things to turn out. These are usually short term goals.

We often think about one or two aspects of a decision but don't look for how our immediate wants have an effect on other people or situations.

If we look at how our decisions help us create our lifestyle and relationships we might make better decisions.

t's not easy to figure out how my thinking helps me make ecisions. How do all of these thoughts and feelings fit together?

Do we sometimes feel like our thoughts are disconnected from our actions? Are there times when our thinking and feelings seem to jump around without order?

I will practice all of the steps of decision making I have practiced so far on this worksheet. Maybe it will help me prepare for important decisions in the future.

Pick a decision with a star from the previous worksheet and write it below in the format provided.

I need/want to _____ because _____

_____. I'm hoping to feel _____ and want

others to _____

_____

Write the information you need to make the decision below.

_____

_____

_____

Write the 3 best choices below and include the most important consequence for each.

1.)
_____

_____

_____

2.)
_____

_____

_____

3.)
_____

_____

_____

Write at least 5 people besides yourself this decision could be important to.

_____

_____

_____

If I practice these steps more times I will get faster and better at doing them.

Pick the other decision with a star and write it below in the format provided.

I need/want to _____ because _____
_____ . I'm hoping to feel _____ and want
others to _____
_____

Write the information you need to make the decision below.
_____
_____
_____

Write the 3 best choices below and include the most important consequence for each.

1.) _____
_____
_____

2.) _____
_____
_____

3.) _____
_____
_____

Write at least 5 people besides yourself this decision could be important to.
_____
_____
_____

If I am going to make the best decisions possible, I must look at how things will turn out. It is best if I do that *before* I make a decision

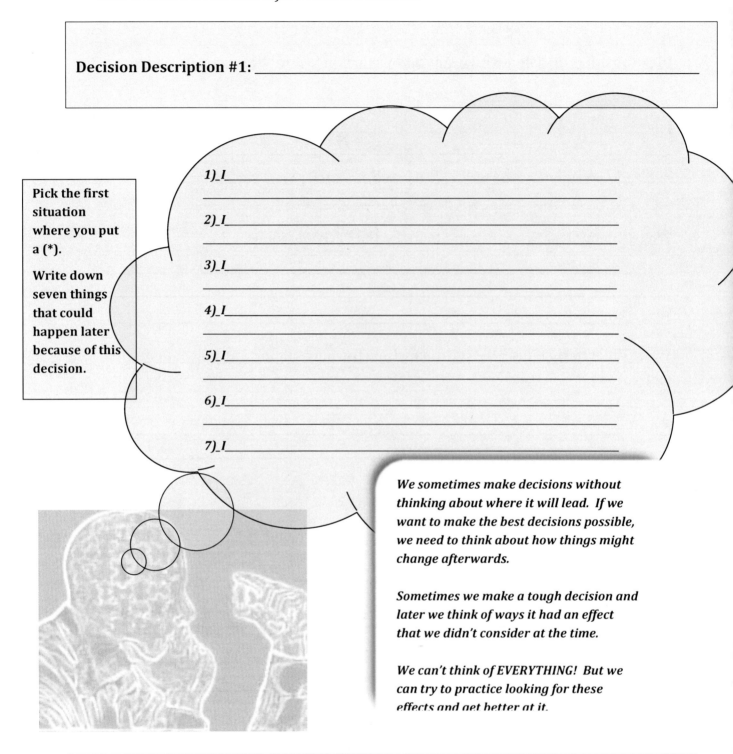

Decision Description #1: _____

Pick the first situation where you put a (*).

Write down seven things that could happen later because of this decision.

1)_I_____
_____

2)_I_____
_____

3)_I_____
_____

4)_I_____
_____

5)_I_____
_____

6)_I_____
_____

7)_I_____

We sometimes make decisions without thinking about where it will lead. If we want to make the best decisions possible, we need to think about how things might change afterwards.

Sometimes we make a tough decision and later we think of ways it had an effect that we didn't consider at the time.

We can't think of EVERYTHING! But we can try to practice looking for these effects and get better at it.

Do we sometimes avoid making hard choices because we are afraid of things we don't know? Do we sometimes make decisions that harm people because we just get tired of trying? If we had a second chance are there some decisions we would make differently?

Decision Description #2: _____

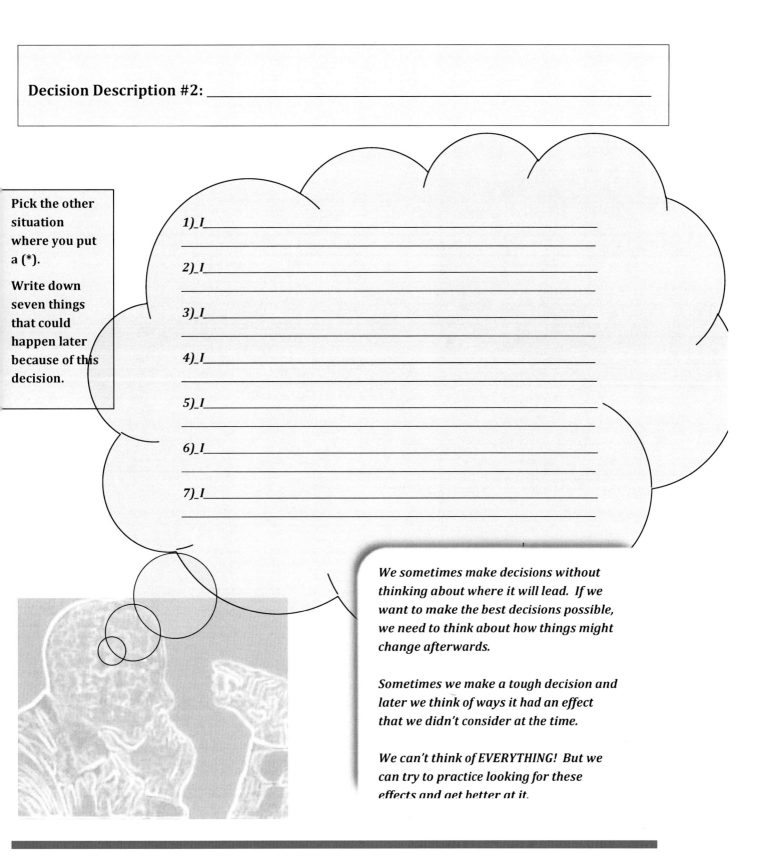

Pick the other situation where you put a (*).

Write down seven things that could happen later because of this decision.

1)_I_____
_____

2)_I_____
_____

3)_I_____
_____

4)_I_____
_____

5)_I_____
_____

6)_I_____
_____

7)_I_____
_____

We sometimes make decisions without thinking about where it will lead. If we want to make the best decisions possible, we need to think about how things might change afterwards.

Sometimes we make a tough decision and later we think of ways it had an effect that we didn't consider at the time.

We can't think of EVERYTHING! But we can try to practice looking for these effects and get better at it.

Do get angry when I make a decision and it doesn't turn out like I wanted? What feelings do I have just before I get angry?

Notes:

Notes:

Step five: Follow Through

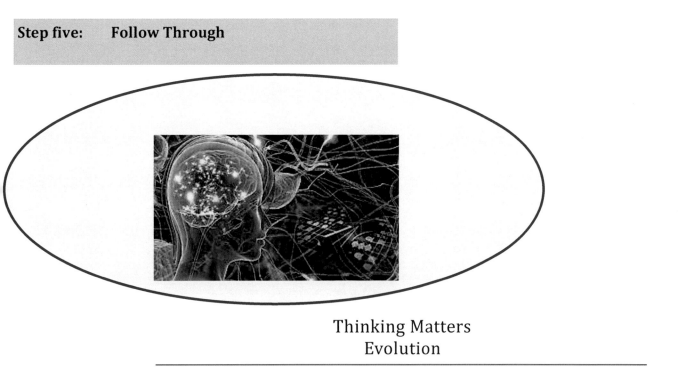

Thinking Matters
Evolution

Step 5 of *Thinking Matters Evolution for Decision Making* helps perform our plan and think about how things turned out for us. Step 5 is where we actually make the decision, do what we think we should and decide if it turned out like we wanted.

Decision Description #1: _____

Write a decision you will make and follow through with. Fill in the lines below as indicated.

1. What action will you take?
2. Where will you take action?
3. Who will be involved
4. What do you want to accomplish?

1)_____
_____
_____

2)_____
_____
_____

3)_____
_____
_____

4)_____
_____
_____

Have we already changed the way we think and believe about something in the past? What are some examples of how we have changed our thinking and attitudes?

Decision Description #1:

_____

Write a decision you will make and follow through with. Fill in the lines below as indicated.

5. What action will you take?
6. Where will you take action?
7. Who will be involved
8. What do you want to accomplish?

1)_____
_____
_____
2)_____
_____
_____

3)_____
_____
_____
4)_____
_____
_____

Do we sometimes avoid making important decisions because we think things could go wrong? Do we sometimes avoid making important decisions because we think others will judge us harshly or argue with us?

Decision Description #2:

_____

1)_____
_____
_____
2)_____
_____
_____

Write the decision you made and followed through with. Fill in the lines below as indicated.

1. What action did you take?
2. Where did you take action?
3. Who was involved
4. What do you accomplish?

3)_____
_____
_____
4)_____
_____
_____

Is it sometimes hard to decide what thinking led to trouble? What makes this a problem for some people? Is it sometimes easier than at other times? What makes one situation different form another? Why is it hard sometimes and easier at other times? Do we sometimes not think we are heading toward trouble when we really ARE?

Decision Description #1:

_____

1)_____

_____

2)_____

_____

_____

Write the decision you made and followed through with. Fill in the lines below as indicated.

1. What action did you take?
2. Where did you take action?
3. Who was involved
4. What do you accomplish?

3)_____

_____

_____

_____

4)_____

_____

_____

_____

Do things sometimes turn out different for others than I thought they would when I make decisions? Are there times when I worry about how other people view me after I have taken action to solve a problem?

Decision Description #1:

_____

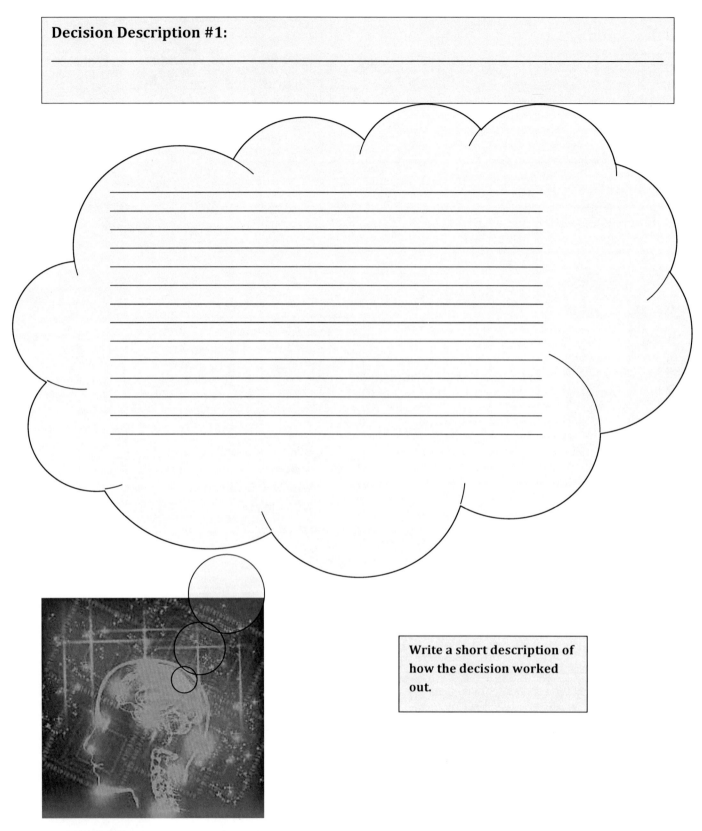

Write a short description of how the decision worked out.

Can I look at past situations and learn how to avoid the same kind of trouble I have had in the past?

Decision Description #1:

_____

List 5 things that might have made things work out better for yourself and others

1)_____

_____

2)_____

_____

3)_____

_____

4)_____

_____

5)_____

_____

Do I spend more time thinking about things that get me into trouble? Or, do I spend more time thinking of ways to avoid trouble?

Some of the things we carry around in our minds are true. Other times we just think they are true because they SEEM true. Things like:

◊ *What we believe*

◊ *Our thoughts*

◊ *Our attitudes*

◊ *What we want*

◊ *Our expectations*

◊ *Our Feelings*

Decision Description #2:

_____

Can I look at past situations and learn how to avoid the same kind of trouble I have had in the past?

Write a short description of how the decision worked out.

Decision Description #2:

_____

List 5 things that might have made things work out better for yourself and others

1)_____
_____

2)_____
_____

3)_____
_____

4)_____
_____

5)_____
_____

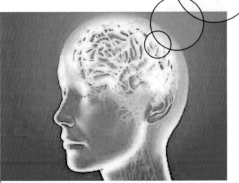

Do I spend more time thinking about things that get me into trouble? Or, do I spend more time thinking of ways to avoid trouble?

Some of the things we carry around in our minds are true. Other times we just think they are true because they SEEM true. Things like:

◊   _What we believe_

◊   _Our thoughts_

◊   _Our attitudes_

◊   _What we want_

◊   _Our expectations_

◊   _Our Feelings_

Notes:

Notes:

Glossary of Terms

Acceptable	Think something is okay or right
Accomplish	Finishing something a person is trying to do.
Accountable	Making sure a person does what they are supposed to do.
Anxious	Feeling restless, eager, worried or nervous.
Brainstorm	Having ideas or suggestions.
Disconnected	Being separate from or cut off from.
Expectation	Thinking something is likely to or should happen.
Evolution	Moving forward and/or develop.
Favorable	Having a hopeful or encouraging situation.
Intend	Having a plan or purpose (for the future).
Interfere	Getting in the way or restricting.
Logic	The way thinking is put together.
Minimize	Making something seem smaller or less important.
Objective	Looking at facts without taking sides or judging.
Outcome	The way things turn out or end up being.
Relationship	Being connected to people or things
Responsibility	Being able to see our own part of something and own it.
Risk	Being likely that something bad might happen.
Pressure	Feeling like something is causing worry or stress.
Separate	Being unattached, isolated or apart from something.
Situation	Being involved in an incident, event or set of facts.
Sullen	Feeling gloomy or having low spirits.
Urgent	Thinking something is very important and there is little time.

Suggested Reading for Criminal Justice Involved

Aos S., Miller M., Drake E. (2006). *Evidence-Based Adult Corrections Programs: What Works and What Does Not. Olympia*. Washington State Institute for Public Policy

Baro, A.L. (1999). "Effects of a Cognitive Restructuring Program on Inmate Institutional Behavior". *Criminal Justice and Behavior*, 26, 466-484.

Bush, J., Bilodeau, B. (1993). Options: A cognitive change program. Longmont, CO: National Institute of Corrections.

Bush, J., Vermont Department of Corrections (2002). A Manual for the Delivery of Cognitive Self-Change, Vermont Department of Corrections, http://doc.vermont.gov/programs

Bush, J., Glick, B., Taymans, J. (1997) Thinking for Change Integrated Cognitive Behavior Change Program. Longmont, CO: National Institute of Corrections.

Bush, J., Criminality and Self Change A Teaching Manual, Longmont, CO: National Institute of Corrections.

Henning, K., & Frueh, B. (1996). Cognitive-behavioral treatment of incarcerated offenders: An evaluation of the Vermont Department of Corrections' cognitive self-change program. Criminal Justice and Behavior, 23, 523-541.

National Institute of Corrections (1997). Cognitive/behavioral strategies to changing offender behavior. Washington, DC: U.S. Department of Justice.

Ross, R., Fabiano, E., & Ross, B. (1986). Reasoning and rehabilitation: A handbook for teaching cognitive skills. University of Ottawa

Gendreau, P., & Andrews, D.A. (1990). Tertiary prevention: What the Meta-Analysis of the Offender Treatment Literature Tells Us About "What Works." Canadian Journal of Criminology, 32, 173-184.

Goldstein, A.P. (1988). *The Prepare Curriculum: Teaching Prosocial Competencies.* Champaign, Illinois: Research Press.

Goldstein, A.P., Glick, B., Reiner, S., Zimmerman, D., & Coultry, T.M. (1987). *Aggression Replacement Training*. Champaign, Illinois: Research Press.

Hubbard D. J., Latessa E.J. (Eds.), (2004). Cincinnati, OH: Center for Criminal Justice Research, University of Cincinnati. Evaluation of Cognitive-Behavioral Programs for Offenders: A Look at Outcome and Responsivity in Five Treatment Programs. Criminal Justice Abstracts database.

Latessa, E.J. (2004). The Challenge of Change: Correctional Programs and Evidence-Based Practices. Criminology & Public Policy, 3(4), 547-559. Criminal Justice Abstracts database.

Wilson D.B., Gallagher C.A., & Mackenzie, D.L. (2000). A Meta-Analysis of Corrections-Based Education, Vocation, and Work Programs for Adult Offenders. Journal of Research in Crime and Delinquency, 37, 347-368.

Withrow, P. (1994). Cognitive restructuring: An approach to dealing with violent inmates. Corrections Today, 56, 112-116.

Yochelson, S., & Samenow, S. (1976). The Criminal Personality: A profile for change. New York: Aronson.

Yochelson, S., & Samenow, S. (1977). The Criminal Personality: The Change Process. New York: Aronson.

Samenow, S.E. (1998). Straight Talk About Criminals. New Jersey. Jason Aronson Inc.

Made in United States
North Haven, CT
08 September 2022

23889482R00033